S0-ASB-570

We are never so lost our angels cannot find us.

Stefanie Raven

FREE BOOKMARK JUST FOR ORDERING

Introducing an all new Angel book with over 50 true-life stories of how God uses His angels to protect and comfort us, stories that will touch your heart.

Angels are everywhere, anyplace you could name from "A" to "Z." They come in response to our prayers—to help us, watch over us and protect us when we need them most.

Organized into 26 alphabetical chapters *ANGELS EVER NEAR: EVERYWHERE FROM A TO Z*, each chapter gives you two stories showing God's angels at work in a specific setting. And each chapter begins with a touching introduction to inspire you with God's love.

COMPLETE THE FREE EXAMINATION CERTIFICATE AND MAIL TODAY FOR YOUR 30-DAY PREVIEW. ➡

No matter where you are, you are never alone. Angels are near you ...

* In the AIR, at the BEDSIDE, in the CITY
* In the EVENING, on the FARM
* On GUARD, on the JOB
* In the NURSERY, in the QUIET
* On the ROADWAY, on VACATION
* In the YARD, and at ZERO hour

ANGELS EVER NEAR brings you into the heart of God's loving care by letting you witness more than four-dozen encounters that can only be explained as angels doing God's work on earth and sending His love. We can never be sure what form God's angels will take - but we CAN be sure they are around us.

Return the Free Examination Certificate today to preview *ANGELS EVER NEAR* for 30-days FREE . . . and receive a FREE bookmark.

NO NEED TO SEND MONEY NOW!

FREE EXAMINATION CERTIFICATE

YES! Rush me *Angels Ever Near - Everywhere From A to Z* at no risk or obligation, to examine FREE for 30 days. If I decide to keep it, I will be billed at the low price of $18.96, payable in two monthly installments of $9.98 each, plus postage and handling. And if not completely satisfied, I may return the book within 30 days and owe nothing. *As a FREE BONUS with each copy, I will receive a beautiful bookmark.*

Total copies ordered: _____

Please print your name and address:

MY NAME _____

MY ADDRESS _____

CITY _____ STATE _____ ZIP _____

❏ Please Bill Me   ❏ Charge My: ❏ MasterCard   ❏ Visa
Credit Card #:

☐☐☐☐ ☐☐☐☐ ☐☐☐☐ ☐☐☐☐   Expiration Date: _____

Signature _____

Allow 4 weeks for delivery. Orders subject to credit approval.
Send no money now. We will bill you later.
www.guidepostsbooks.com

Printed in USA
011/201870134

BUSINESS REPLY MAIL
FIRST-CLASS MAIL PERMIT NO. 38 CARMEL NY
POSTAGE WILL BE PAID BY ADDRESSEE

IDEALS PUBLICATIONS
A Division of GUIDEPOSTS
PO BOX 797
CARMEL NY 10512-9905

NO POSTAGE
NECESSARY
IF MAILED
IN THE
UNITED STATES

Go back in time . . .
with *Memories of Times Past*

Now, in this beautiful book from Ideals, experience wonderful sights, stories, poems, recipes and songs that will stir your soul and take you back to your own MEMORIES OF TIMES PAST.

From the moment you open the front cover, you will be transported back to the world of your youth with wonderful stories and poems about family and home, one-room schoolhouses and friends, neighborhood gatherings and parties, with old-fashioned recipes like Mama used to make and pastimes from an age gone by. This beautiful book is illustrated with vintage sepia-tinted photographs, magazine advertisements for products from the past, and exquisite antique rooms.

160 pages, full color throughout, heavy-weight enamel stock, deluxe hardcover binding.

There are photos and paintings, all with that warm, golden glow of times past. Family stories and poems, some humorous, some tender, all so delightful that you may long for a return to the values of yesteryear.

If you love the past with all of its charm . . . if you love to remember a gentler and slower time . . . if you love the old-time music with its memories . . . and if you enjoy reading the stories and poems of a bygone time . . . you owe it to yourself to take advantage of our offer.

Return the Free Examination Certificate today to preview MEMORIES OF TIMES PAST for 30-days FREE . . . and receive FREE VINATAGE POSTCARDS just for ordering.

FREE EXAMINATION CERTIFICATE

YES! I'd like to examine *Memories of Times Past* for 30-days FREE. If after 30 days I am not delighted with it, I may return it and owe nothing. If I decide to keep it, I will be billed $24.95, plus postage and handling. In either case, the FREE Vintage postcards are mine to keep.

Please print your name and address:

_____
MY NAME
_____
MY ADDRESS
_____
CITY   STATE   ZIP

Total copies ordered _____
❏ Please Bill Me ❏ Charge My: ❏ MasterCard ❏ Visa

Credit Card #:   Expiration Date: _____
                                        Signature _____

Allow 4 weeks for delivery. Orders subject to credit approval.
Send no money now. We will bill you later.
www.IdealsBook.com

015/201870146

COMPLETE THE FREE EXAMINATIO[N]
CERTIFICATE AND MAIL TODAY
FOR YOUR 30-DAY PREVIEW.

NO NEED TO SEND MONEY NOW

ideals®
MOTHER'S DAY

More Than 50 Years of Celebrating Life's Most Treasured Moments

Vol. 59, No. 2

Sweet May hath come to love us.
—Heinrich Heine

IDEALS—Vol. 59, No. 2 March MMII IDEALS (ISSN 0019-137X, USPS 256-240)
is published six times a year: January, March, May, July, September, and November by
IDEALS PUBLICATIONS, a division of Guideposts
39 Seminary Hill Road, Carmel, NY 10512.

Printed on Weyerhaeuser Husky. The paper used in this publication meets the minimum requirements of
American National Standard for Information Sciences—
Permanence of Paper for Printed Library Materials, ANSI Z39.48-1984.

Periodicals postage paid at Carmel, New York, and additional mailing offices.
POSTMASTER: Send address changes to Ideals, 39 Seminary Hill Road, Carmel, NY 10512.
For subscription or customer service questions, contact Ideals Publications,
a division of Guideposts, 39 Seminary Hill Road, Carmel, NY 10512. Fax 845-228-2115.

Reader Preference Service: We occasionally make our mailing lists available to
other companies whose products or services might interest you.
If you prefer not to be included, please write to Ideals Customer Service.

ISBN 0-8249-1200-4 GST 893989236

Visit *Ideals'* website at www.idealsbooks.com

Cover Photo: Yellow roses, Lancaster, Pennsylvania. Larry Lefever/Grant Heilman Photography.
Inside Front Cover: SUMMER DREAMS. Mary Kay Krell, artist.
Inside Back Cover: MOTHER AND CHILD WITH ORANGE. Julius Gari Melchers, artist.
Peter Harholdt/Superstock.

May

Elsie Grant

The violets are blooming. The robins greet the dawn.
The south and west winds whisper across the greening lawn.
All April's tears forgotten, all April's smiles as well,
Now May's laid warm hands on the earth and cast a magic spell.

And everywhere unfurling, buds open in the sun.
The sap of life is stirring. Now winter's sleep is done.
From every pond and river the frogs sing roundelays:
A welcoming to springtime; a chorus in its praise.

Tranquility

Dorothy Bailey Spofford

I look at a green world waking
On a morn that is almost May.
The spring is mine for the taking,
And the dream is here to stay.

I look at a light just breaking
With the hyacinth breath of dawn,
And an early celebrant raking
New grass on a pearly lawn.

The dream and the magic are shaking
My heart in its dormant breast
While all the old doubts are forsaking
And leaving my soul at rest.

*Irises follow a curved fencerow in Door County,
Wisconsin. Photo by Daniel Dempster.*

From a Tower in May

Myrtella Southerland

A tower I know, ah, far away
In springtime where the breezes play,
O'er which the heavens, deeply blue,
Shine softly in their lovely hue,
Where robins jubilantly sing
And skylarks, gaily on the wing,
Pause oft to warble and declare
New England here is very fair.

The picturesque, the peaceful scene,
The noble trees, so fresh and green,
The tumbling rocks, the view afar,
How wonderful these beauties are!
Oh, therefore he who in delight
May dream sometimes at such a height
Above the world, its sordid dust,
Must feel its richer joy and trust!

What ideals must be his to know
Who pauses here, the earth below
Spread like a picture at his feet!
Arbutus blooming fresh and sweet

Must tell him that the May once more
Waits, like a comrade, at his door
To walk with him, where'er he would,
O'er hills and vales or through the wood.

Who dwells in lofty heights like this
Must truly know a deeper bliss
Than he who seeks no noble height
In which to grow and find new sight.
He must be nobler than the soul
Who dreams no dreams, who seeks no goal.
He must be kind; he must be strong,
His heart a sweet and lilting song.

So would I find for me a tower
In which to bide a quiet hour
And ponder o'er the beauteous things
Of which the skylark sings and sings,
Dream out the songs to help a friend
To some dear, cherished, longed-for end,
And think of all my blessings here
Upon this golden hemisphere.

Left: Pride of Madeira blooms along the headlands above California's Big Sur Coast. Photo by Terry Donnelly. Overleaf: Pansies and azaleas circle a lush lawn at Callaway Gardens in Pine Mountain, Georgia. Photo by William H. Johnson/Johnson's Photography.

Golden Bells

Ruth B. Field

Small golden bells in the sun are ringing
In tune with birds across the blue skies winging.
Each one upon its slender stalk is swaying
And trembles with the message it is saying.
Go find a verdant little mossy hollow
Where sweet white violet fragrance you will follow,
And here you'll find as small gold bells are swinging
You cannot help but join them in their singing.
Little bells of gold midst mottled leaves
Bring joy to every heart that believes
They have a sweet carillon to sing—
The fulfilled promise of another spring.

The Lady in the Florist Shop

Ruth Hudson

I asked for yellow violets.
She said, "I never saw a yellow violet.
I didn't know there were such things.
I thought that violets were blue, or maybe white."

But I remember childhood springs
When I picked handfuls of gold violets
And put them in a little vase I had
Along with wild fern fronds, just then uncurled.
They were so beautiful!

I think it's sad she doesn't know
About the yellow violets,
Nor saw them blooming on a spring-swept hill.
For all her flowers, I would not change with her;
For I remember yellow violets still.

Border: Ferns carpet the woodland floor. Left: Dogtooth violets add their golden touch to the greenery. Photos by Dwight Kuhn.

Unforgotten

Madison J. Cawein

How many things, that we would remember,
Sweet or sad, or great or small,
Do our minds forget! And how one thing only,
One little thing endures o'er all!
For many things have I forgotten,
But this one thing can never forget—
The scent of a primrose, woodland wet,
Long years ago I found in a far land;
A fragile flower that April set,
Rainy pink, in her forehead's garland.

How many things by the heart are forgotten!
Sad as sweet, or little or great!
And how one thing that could mean nothing
Stays knocking still at the heart's red gate!

*The flowers we most love are those
we knew when we were very young.
when our senses were most acute . . .
and our natures most lyrical.*

                    -Dorothy Thompson

Spring Sonnet

Reginald Holmes

I've never known a spring like this before,
Though I have seen so many come and go.
The violets show in lovely purple clusters,
And every cherry branch like drifts of snow.
The yellow jonquils nod to passing strangers
While lilacs fill the air with rich perfume.
The tulip bulbs that slept have now awakened
And line the walk with dazzling crimson bloom.

Other springs, I had not viewed your loveliness
Or thought that you were more than passing fair;
But now, with bridal wreath in bloom beside you
And stray, white petals nestling in your hair,
Like song birds on the wing, my spirits soar;
I've never known a spring like this before!

The nightingale appear'd the first,
And as her melody she sang,
The apple into blossom burst,
To life the grass and violets sprang.

—Heinrich Heine

A single gold blossom rises among the fallen petals in Door County, Wisconsin. Photo by Darryl R. Beers.

Tidings of
Invisible Things

William Wordsworth

I have seen
A curious child, who dwelt upon a tract
Of inland ground, applying to his ear
The convolutions of a smooth-lipped shell;
To which, in silence hushed, his very soul
Listened intensely; for from within were heard
Murmurings, whereby the monitor expressed
Mysterious union with its native sea.
Even such a shell the universe itself
Is to the ear of faith; and there are times,
I doubt not, when to you it doth impart
Authentic tidings of invisible things,
Of ebb and flow, and ever-during power,
And central peace, subsisting at the heart
Of endless agitation.

*Evening light hits the dune grasses and sand on Michigan's Sleeping
Bear Dunes National Lakeshore. Photo by Mary Liz Austin.*

From My Garden Journal

Lisa Ragan

LADY'S MANTLE

My mother's hazel eyes twinkle with delight whenever she admires a new flower blossom in her garden, and I often present her with an armful of fresh flowers on Mother's Day just to see her eyes dance in appreciation. If the weather is agreeable, Mom then guides me through her own garden, where we catch up on family news as she tosses various foliage and flower buds into the ready basket she often carries. Back in her kitchen, I watch in amazement as she creates a stunning bouquet by carefully selecting buds and greenery from the basket to complement whatever blossoms I brought. If an especially warm spring has inspired some early blossoms, then Mom often adds sprigs of an old-fashioned plant called lady's mantle throughout the bouquet. Those airy sprays of chartreuse fluff always make her arrangements sparkle with color, just as her eyes dance and sparkle when she steps back to appraise the finished bouquet.

I first learned of lady's mantle from my mother, whose

Aunt Edna had traveled to England and fallen in love with traditional English cottage gardens. Aunt Edna especially loved lady's mantle, a staple of cottage gardens, and she soon learned to grow it in her own garden back in America. The common name for this charming plant, lady's mantle, has been attributed to different legends, including one that tells of a garland of lady's mantle that was placed on the Virgin Mary and then named in her honor. Another story argues that the plant became called lady's mantle because its fan-shaped leaves with their ruffled edges resemble tiny maidens' cloaks. Mother says that Aunt Edna enjoyed both legends and often repeated the tales when she welcomed guests to her garden.

The botanical name for lady's mantle, *alchemilla*, provides a clue to the plant's history. The word *alchemilla* derives from alchemy, which was a type of medieval science. The alchemists of the Middle Ages focused on transforming base metals into gold as well as trying to find a universal cure for all diseases. Alchemists carefully collected the precious dewdrops from the leaves of the lady's mantle to use in their elixirs. They prized the dewdrops as having healing properties and used them as an essential ingredient in their work. Although the alchemists were never successful in their aims to create the ultimate panacea, *alchemilla*'s healing properties were recorded in 1548 by pharmacists who noted "Our Ladies' Mantel," *alchemilla vulgaris,* to be a superior herb for treating wounds. The larger form of lady's mantle, *alchemilla mollis,* was introduced to the Western world from its native Turkey in 1874 and has come to be regarded as the classic lady's mantle.

A herbaceous perennial, lady's mantle features velvety soft, gray-green leaves with wavy edges; its mounding foliage grows from eight to twelve inches tall and can reach up to eighteen inches in diameter. Delicate flower clusters in an almost fluorescent lime-green color bloom above the foliage in late spring or early summer and last for several weeks. Lady's mantle blossoms make exceptional cut flowers and can also be dried for later use. Although the blooms are indeed striking, many gardeners grow lady's mantle primarily for its exquisite foliage, which remains vibrant long after the last blossoms have fallen. If the plant appears somewhat spent after flowering, cutting it back will encourage a fresh crop of new leaves that will thrive well into autumn.

Dedicated gardeners since the time of the medieval alchemists have recorded the beauty of the diamond-like raindrops or dewdrops often adorning the leaves of lady's mantle. Tiny hairs on the foliage capture the drops in perfect spheres, but they are often not raindrops or dewdrops at all. Lady's mantle has a unique way of expelling excess water from the roots up through the leaves, which is why it often sparkles with shimmering wet drops long after every other plant in the garden has dried.

Although *alchemilla mollis* is generally considered the classic lady's mantle, gardeners can sometimes still find *alchemilla vulgaris,* which produces a slightly smaller plant with greener flowers and smoother leaves. A similar species, *alchemilla alpina* (mountain mantle), produces a small plant that has neat green leaves with silver edges and green flowers. An even smaller version that reaches heights of no more than eight inches, *alchemilla faroensis* "Pumila," is called dwarf lady's mantle and includes chartreuse flowers similar to the full-size version. *Alchemilla mollis,* the "Thriller" cultivar, features the cele-brated gray-green leaves and starry chartreuse flowers with a straw-like texture.

Lady's mantle grows well in full sun to partial shade throughout much of the central and northern United States. The plant may require afternoon shade in warmer climates and full sun in cooler climates for optimum growth. Seeds will germinate when sown in moist, rich soil and should be planted approximately eighteen inches apart in spring. Lady's mantle may wilt if subjected to intense heat or humidity and does not grow well in wet areas. With its unique gray-green foliage, the plant can provide a beautiful edging to the garden or add an accent of color below shrubs and tall flowers. In shady areas, lady's mantle can even be used as a groundcover. Propagation of the plant can be achieved easily—too easily in some climates. Although it is a self-sowing plant, aggressive naturalization can be controlled by diligently removing spent flowers before they have a chance to spread their seed. Mature lady's mantle plants can also be divided in spring, if desired. This hardy plant resists most pests and diseases, although it can succumb to fungus in overly wet or humid conditions.

This spring has brought us enough warm weather to inspire some early flowers from Mom's own lady's mantle plants. With her own bouquet complete and plenty of blossoms to spare, we decide to create a second arrangement to take to Grandma. I put on another pot of peppermint tea as Mom seeks out the perfect vase. As I pour two more cups of tea, I smile and think that this is indeed a befitting way to celebrate two special ladies in my life on Mother's Day—with their own posies of lady's mantle.

Lisa Ragan tends her small but mighty city garden in Nashville, Tennessee, with the help of her two shih-tzu puppies, Clover and Curry.

There Is So Much to Do

Edna Jaques

There is so much to do in May—
Fields to be plowed and trees to spray,
Bushes to prune, a straggly row
Of berries to thin out and to hoe,
A weedy lawn to roll and rake,
A special flower bed to make.

A day to just walk round about,
A day to fish for speckled trout,
An hour to watch new leaves uncurl,
A day to watch the swallows whirl
Across the fields in crazy flight,
A sky that's full of stars at night.

And, oh, I must make time somehow
To stand and watch a farmer plow,
Turning the furrows straight and neat,
Or watch him sow a field of wheat
And listen while a robin trills
A love song older than the hills.

And, oh, I must remember to
Hunt for wild mint around the slough.
It grows so lush and fragrant there;
I must take time to breathe the air
Laden with blossoms and perfume
And old trees bursting into bloom.

Oh, please take a short time for play;
Life is so beautiful in May.

*Lupine flowers soften a field in San Luis Obispo,
California. Photo by Londie G. Padelsky.*

Kitchen Gods

Jean Rasey

An oven was her joy, she often said,
Baking away her time with tart and bread
While spoons that never held a bit too much
Combined the flour and spice with measured touch.
And yet no recipe could match the sense
Of something wistful, vital, and intense
That filled her mind; the spark that gave her wings
And flamed her thoughts to bright imaginings.
In youth, 'twas how to feed a hungry man;
The golden loaf that steamed upon the pan
In fragrant rippling waves concealed a need
Within a heart that love had never freed.

In her domain, a kitchen dressed with charm,
She mixed her dreams of might and brawny arm,
Portioning time away with paste and bun
Until one day she knew her youth was done;
The paste and bun and coffee freshly brewed
Became her love and, like a lover, wooed
New friends; and through her yeast and spice and dough
She found the greatest romance life could know.

A friendly kitchen feeds both hunger and spirit. Photo by Jessie Walker.

Remember When

MOTHER'S APRON

Marjorie Holmes

There was a good excuse for aprons in our mothers' day. In that blissful pre-cholesterol era, hardly anybody broiled or pressure-cooked; no, foods were fried lengthily, smokily, often sputteringly, in good old-fashioned lard.

To bake a cake, you didn't simply open a package and make a few absentminded gestures with an electric mixer. You coped long and lovingly with flour and eggs and maybe clabbered milk, pausing for good measure to shake down the ashes in the old coal range, smash more kindling across your knees, and shovel in more cobs or chunks of rich, black, dusty coal. An apron was not only part of a woman's uniform of domesticity; it was protection.

Mothers continued to prepare for their day's assault upon the premises by donning layer upon layer of garments, culminating with a "housedress." A "housedress" might be vaguely pretty, with a bow or a few buttons on it, but mostly it was plain, functional, and washable, with all elements of character or imagination reduced to the absolute minimum.

The costume was then crowned with a dustcap. The cap was often plain sturdy gingham to match the dress. Or it might be a perky concoction of lace and ribbon rosettes. In any case, it served the purpose of protecting the hair from the dust that mothers whacked or shook or swept from the house.

And always, as a kind of extra fortification from all this, a mother wore an apron. She put it on over her housedress in the morning, and she didn't remove it until she cleaned up for the afternoon. Then, like as not, she donned a fresh one from her ample stock.

Women were better organized then, perhaps because they had to be. They seldom had a car in the driveway to whisk them off to meetings or the super-market while the clothes washed and dried. My mother certainly never did the impulse cleaning to which I'm prone, nor popped a pie in the oven or started ironing after dark. As with her neighbors, each day was sacred to its appointed tasks—the laundry, the baking, the scrubbing; what's more, she rose early, accomplished the scheduled undertaking, and was ready for the sacred rite of making herself presentable by two o'clock. (To be "caught dirty" any time after three would have been sheer disgrace.)

This involved at least a sponge bath with a kettle of cistern water heated on the stove, the neat doing-up of hair with a number of pins and tortoiseshell combs, putting on a "good" dress as opposed to a housedress, and silk instead of cotton stockings, finishing off with a touch of rice powder and a dab of cologne. She was then ready for any callers who might drop in; or she'd lie down with the latest installment of a Kathleen Norris serial.

This brief span during the afternoon was the only time she was minus an apron. And when she arose to start supper, did she change, as we are wont to, into something comfortable if sloppy? No, indeed, she simply protected her daintiness with a nice fresh apron. Sometimes a big apron that encircled her neck like loving arms; sometimes one that tied at the waist in a bow that brothers or your dad would yank when they wanted to tease her. If company was coming, it would be a fancy apron, all organdy frills, the kind women still wear for serving dinners and sociables at the church. But family apron or company apron, it was always crisp and pretty and clean, and she often wore it to the table.

Frequently she continued to wear it on into the evening after the dishes were done. Standing at the back fence visiting with a neighbor, strolling about

A future chef learns to make a favorite treat in this vintage image from H. Armstrong Roberts.

the yard to see about her flowers, or sitting on the porch in the twilight watching the children playing redlight or catching fireflies in a jar. And if the air were chilly, she wrapped her arms in her apron to keep them warm.

An apron was a part of Mother—like her laugh or her eyes or her big black pocketbook. And it was more than her protection against the hazards of cooking and keeping house—it was a kind of protection for you as well. It was big enough to shelter you too sometimes if you were cold. There was always a handkerchief for you in one of its roomy pockets. It was a part of her lap.

And her apron gave you assurance. Rushing in from school or play, even if you didn't see or hear her, you felt better just finding that apron hanging behind the kitchen door or dangling across a chair. Her apron, smelling of cookies and starch and Mother. It comforted you. It made you feel secure.

Maybe that's why our youngsters instinctively want us to own aprons. Lots of aprons. And to wear one now and then. Why we ourselves can't resist buying them at bazaars. Maybe we still feel the strong, sweet tug of apron strings. We remember the time when an apron meant a lap to be cuddled on, a pocket with a hanky to wipe your nose on, someone who cared about you. The days when a mother's apron symbolized love!

Ideals' Family Recipes

To many of us, a favorite childhood memory involves licking the bowl as Mother baked our favorite cake. Whether the cake was chocolate or coconut, the smiles were the same; and for the rest of our lives, no one will be able to follow that recipe quite like Mom. We would love to try your favorite recipe too. Send a typed copy to Ideals Publications, 535 Metroplex Drive, Suite 250, Nashville, TN 37211. We pay $10 for each recipe published.

My Mother's Chocolate Cake
Judy Tutor of Molina, Colorado

2 teaspoons baking soda
½ cup milk
2 cups all-purpose flour
½ cup cocoa
1 teaspoon salt
½ cup butter
1½ cups granulated sugar
2 eggs
1 teaspoon vanilla
1 cup hot water

Preheat oven to 350° F. In a small bowl, dissolve baking soda in milk. Set aside. In a medium bowl, sift together flour, cocoa, and salt. Set aside. In a large bowl, cream butter with sugar. Add eggs, vanilla, and milk mixture; mix well. Slowly stir in dry ingredients until well blended. Add hot water and mix well. Pour batter into a 9-by-13-by-2-inch greased and floured pan. Bake 25 to 35 minutes or until toothpick inserted into the center comes out clean. Makes 8 servings.

Raspberry Cake
Terri Colledge of Breezewood, Pennsylvania

2 cups all-purpose flour
2 teaspoons baking powder
1 teaspoon salt
½ cup shortening
1½ cups granulated sugar
2 eggs
1¼ cups milk
1 pint raspberries

Preheat oven to 350° F. In a medium bowl, sift together flour, baking powder, and salt. Set aside. In a large bowl, cream together shortening and sugar. Add eggs and milk and mix well. Slowly stir in dry ingredients; mix well. Fold in raspberries. Pour batter into a greased bundt pan. Bake 35 to 45 minutes or until toothpick inserted into the center comes out clean. Makes 8 servings.

Grandma's Cheesecake

Eleanore Kearney of Shoreham, New York

1   cup shortbread cookie crumbs
2   tablespoons butter, melted
1   cup plus 1 tablespoon granulated sugar
3   8-ounce packages cream cheese, softened
4   large eggs

1   pint sour cream
2   tablespoons all-purpose flour
2   teaspoons vanilla
1   teaspoon lemon juice
1   cup heavy whipping cream

Preheat oven to 325° F. Grease the bottom and sides of a 10-inch springform pan. In a small bowl, combine cookie crumbs, butter, and 1 tablespoon of the sugar. Pat down firmly in bottom of springform pan to make crust. Place pan in freezer while preparing filling. In a large bowl, beat cream cheese with remaining sugar until well blended. Add remaining ingredients one at a time, beating well after each addition. Pour mixture into prepared pan and bake 20 minutes. Lower oven temperature to 300° F and bake an additional 40 minutes. Turn off oven and allow cake to cool in oven with door closed for 1 hour. Cool at room temperature before placing in refrigerator. Makes 8 servings.

Coconut Cream Cheese Pound Cake

Lou O. Knight of Forest, Mississippi

3   cups all-purpose flour
1   teaspoon baking soda
¼   teaspoon salt
½   cup butter, softened
½   cup shortening
1   8-ounce package cream cheese, softened

3   cups granulated sugar
6   eggs
1   teaspoon vanilla
1   teaspoon coconut flavoring
1   6-ounce package frozen coconut, thawed

Preheat oven to 350° F. In a medium bowl, sift together flour, baking soda, and salt. Set aside. In an extra-large bowl, cream butter, shortening, and cream cheese with an electric mixer. Gradually add sugar, mixing until light and fluffy. Add eggs one at a time, beating after each addition. Add vanilla and coconut flavoring; mix well. Slowly add dry ingredients, stirring with spoon just until blended. Stir in coconut. Spoon batter into a greased and floured bundt pan. Bake 1 hour and 15 minutes or until a toothpick inserted into the middle comes out clean. Makes 8 servings.

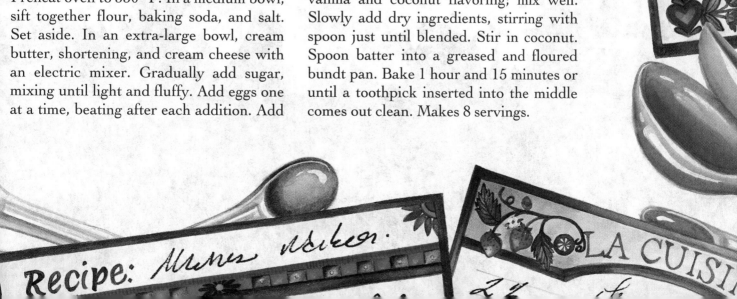

Motherhood
Margaret Rorke

In her arms a generation
Is held lovingly from birth.
In her eyes there's adoration
And assurance of its worth.

From her tongue is heard the teaching
Of its heritage and hope,
And her hands coax forth its reaching
For the infinite in scope.

She's its ever present model.
She's its fortress, faith, and food

From the time it starts to toddle
Till with age it is imbued.

She's the confidante and healer
Of the wounds to which it's heir
And the pard'nable revealer
Of the best it has to bear.

Every time God's sought assistance
For some purpose wholly good,
With the breath of its existence
He's entrusted motherhood.

Mother's Day
Esther Kem Thomas

Anything that puts one in
A fervent, prayerful mood,
Or stirs the good in men, or tends
The fires of gratitude,
Or wakes in him attention to
The keeping of his brother
Is pictured, in a worldly way,
As tribute to a mother!

Any act of tolerance
Or patient faith to be
Is tribute to the faith I know
A mother had in me.

Any good I may achieve
Is fostered by another.
What she expects of me, I'll try
To be it, for my mother!

Help us, then, by word and deed,
Fulfill her expectation;
For, born of mothers, is the fate
Of home and state and nation.
There's hope for worlds made up of men
Who, dealing with each other,
Forget not God and tolerance,
Remembering a mother!

A May basket holds a bouquet of springtime. Photo by Gay Bumgarner.

A Mother's Joy

Thelma Belle McCoy

With joy my son runs in to plea,
"Mother, Mother, come and see."
And though my hands are deep in dishes,
I think it fun to heed his wishes.

For I have learned through motherhood
That children share so much that's good.
They see the things we overlook.
Expectantly, his hand I took.

And I stooped down beside my son
To watch the ants as, one by one,
They deftly moved some grains of sand
And carried them across our land.

We gazed in awe and felt a thrill.
Those grains of sand became a hill!
And in the place where they had laid,
The pathway to a home was made.

It's said the child will lead you.
And for myself, I know it's true.
Each time my child says, "Come and see,"
The hand of God has reached to me.

*A brick path through a garden leads to
home. Photo by Jessie Walker.*

In Storybook Land

Virginia Katherine Oliver

In storybook land there is magic,
With the power to take you away
From worries and cares all about you
And the problems you face every day.
There is mystery, romance, and humor
Hidden within every book.
Wonderful thoughts are awaiting inside,
If you just take a moment to look.
Just wander away in your fancy
To the days of the long, long ago,
Or to glorious worlds of make-believe
Where breezes of dreamland do blow.
Once under the spell of its magic,
You will then evermore understand
What it means to leave this world behind
And sail off to storybook land.

Twilight Stories

James Whitcomb Riley

Neither daylight, starlight, moonlight,
But a sad-sweet term of some light
By the saintly name of twilight.

The Grandma twilight stories! Still
A childish listener, I hear
The katydid and whippoorwill,
In deepening atmosphere

Of velvet dusk, blent with the low,
Soft music of the voice that sings
And tells me tales of long ago
And old enchanted things.

While far fails the last dim daylight,
And the fireflies in the twilight
Drift about like flakes of starlight.

A delicate garden provides a spot for storytime in Portrait of a Mother and Daughter Reading a Book *by artist Edwin Harris. Image from Christie's Images.*

LEGENDARY AMERICANS

Nancy Skarmeas

MCRAE

DR. SEUSS

Dr. Seuss and his books are so familiar to us all that we are apt to take him for granted. Some weary parents, upon what seems like the millionth reading of *The Cat in the Hat* to an eager toddler, might even harbor a momentary feeling of resentment toward the prolific author and his cat in the red-striped hat. But put *The Cat in the Hat* in the hands of a beginning reader, a child just on the verge of unlocking the mystery of the written word, and the magic of Dr. Seuss will become apparent again. These fledgling readers are Seuss's true audience. Their smiles of amusement and accomplishment as they master each page reveal

the truly marvelous achievement of the inimitable Dr. Seuss.

Theodor Seuss Geisel did not set out to become a writer of children's books. He did not, in fact, actually set out to become anything in particular. Born in Springfield, Massachusetts, in 1904, Geisel was a bright, creative child who grew into a bright and creative young man in search of the proper outlet for his talents. He attended Dartmouth College, where he was a good student but less devoted to pure academics than to his work for the campus humor magazine. It was while at Dartmouth that Geisel began signing his work with his middle name, "Seuss." After Dartmouth, Geisel went to England and Oxford University, where upon enrollment he envisioned studying to become a professor of English literature. He quite soon found advanced literary studies too dry for his tastes, however, and often whiled away long lectures drawing cartoons in his notebooks. On the advice of his good friend Helen Palmer, Geisel left Oxford and spent two years traveling through Europe. He returned to the United States in 1927 and that same year made Helen Palmer his wife.

Geisel made his living in the years that followed by drawing cartoons and writing essays for humor magazines. He also began doing some writing and cartooning for advertising. He added the honorary title of doctor to his old Dartmouth pseudonym and began signing his work "Dr. Seuss."

Oddly enough, it was while onboard a ship sailing from France to New York that Ted Geisel had the inspiration that would launch his career as a writer of children's books. During the long, quiet hours of the crossing, when the only sound was the rhythmic droning of the ship's engines, Geisel found his mind creating words to the engine's rhythm. He arrived home with a recurring rhyme in his head: "And that is a story that no one can beat, and to think that I saw it on Mulberry Street." Upon the suggestion of his wife, Geisel determined to write a story based upon that rhyme. Twenty-eight publishers turned down Geisel's story, most describing it as "too different" to be marketable. Geisel might have given up on the story altogether if not for a chance encounter with an old Dartmouth friend who had recently begun working in children's publishing. The old friend took on the book as a favor to Geisel. *And to Think That I Saw It on Mulberry Street* was published in 1937.

The "too different" *Mulberry Street* received great critical praise for its originality and achieved moderate sales success: enough to launch Dr. Seuss's career in children's books, but not enough to convince him to abandon all other pursuits. While Geisel published three more books for children in the years that followed, each one continuing the development of his unique style, with distinctive drawings of imaginary characters, wonderful, simple rhythms, and an amusing vocabulary of nonsense names and words, he also continued his work in advertising. During World War II, Geisel served in the army as a member of the Signal Corps and made animated movies and documentaries. Two of those documentaries won Oscars for Geisel. In the 1940s and 50s, Ted Geisel was an ambitious, energetic, and creative man who still had not found one consuming project.

It was in 1957 that Geisel came upon the challenge that would define his career and earn him a place among the great names of American children's literature. After reading an article about the problems American students were having with early reading skills, in which the author blamed in great part the uninspiring *Dick and Jane* readers for turning students away from reading, Geisel determined to write a new type of book for the beginning reader. His publisher supplied him with a list of 225 words that beginning readers should learn. Working from that list, Geisel created *The Cat in the Hat.* Geisel himself later explained the genesis of the book. After much trial and error, he said, "I was desperate, so I decided to read [the 225 words] once more. The first two words that rhymed would be the title of my book and I would go from there. I found 'cat' and then I found 'hat.' That's genius, you see!"

The Cat in the Hat, of course, was an unprecedented success and spawned an entire series of early reader books by Dr. Seuss. Ted and Helen Geisel also began a publishing group devoted solely to beginning readers. Their concept was simple yet, given the books available at the time, revolutionary. Using restricted vocabulary lists, repetitive language, descriptive illustrations, and a sense of imagination and fun, Dr. Seuss's books aimed to make learning to read a pleasure. The idea seemed obvious enough at the time; but today, among the masses of early reader books in print, few achieve anything near Geisel's appeal.

The key to Dr. Seuss's success was Ted Geisel's wonderful imagination, which never surrendered itself fully to sober adulthood. Writing books for children was a business for Geisel, but he never lost his sense of fun. One of his most beloved books, *Green Eggs and Ham,* was written on a dare. A friend bet Geisel that he could not create a book using only fifty words. Geisel took up the challenge and produced a book that has been read and enjoyed by millions of children for nearly fifty years.

Along with his early reader books, Geisel continued to write books for older children, books which have become some of the most beloved read-aloud stories in the English language. He often used these books as a forum for social messages about tolerance and sharing and kindness. But while *The Lorax, The Sneetches,* and *The Grinch Who Stole Christmas* may come with messages, they also come with the distinctly Seussian sense of fun and imagination. The words of Dr. Seuss are too clever and engaging to ever sound like sermonizing.

Dr. Seuss's many wonderful characters have become instantly recognizable icons in American culture, an industry all their own, with toys and movies and reprint after reprint. But the real value of Dr. Seuss to our children remains quite simple and needs no marketing or merchandising. Adult, accomplished readers might not remember what it feels like to first unlock the great mystery of the written word, nor can they remember the great frustration that can come with the effort or the pride and excitement that follow success. Dr. Seuss's books take the fledgling reader by the hand and welcome him with a wink and a laugh. A child who turns the last page of *The Cat in the Hat* or *Hop on Pop* or *Green Eggs and Ham* and proudly says, "I read it myself," is always eager for more reading. Not because his parents want him to read, or because his teacher is telling him to read, but because, thanks to Dr. Seuss, he knows reading can be a magical adventure.

TRAVELER'S
Diary

DR. SEUSS NATIONAL MEMORIAL
SPRINGFIELD, MASSACHUSETTS

Christine Landry

I still remember lying in bed, with covers pulled up to my chin, and looking at my mother as she read from *Green Eggs and Ham* with its shiny, orange cover: "That Sam-I-am! That Sam-I-am! I do not like that Sam-I-am!" And when I got older, I can recall one December hearing my mother read to my younger brother from *How the Grinch Stole Christmas* as the Grinch with his heart "two sizes too small" stuffed Christmas trees up a chimney. As I matured, and seemingly grew too old for such books, Dr. Seuss still remained a part of my life. In high school, my friends and I performed *The Cat in the Hat* in French for a class project; and when I graduated, my parents gave me a copy of *Oh, the Places You'll Go!* So when I visited Springfield, Massachusetts, recently, I made a trip to the future site of the Dr. Seuss National Memorial, which will be completed in June of this year. What I discovered there was a piece of land dedicated to honoring a well-loved literary personality and to encouraging reading, especially among children.

Theodor Geisel's hometown of Springfield greatly influenced the ideas and characters that would later fill the pages of his books. In *And to Think That I Saw It on Mulberry Street* (the first book published under Geisel's alter ego, Dr. Seuss), his drawings appear as playful versions of actual houses situated on Springfield's Mulberry Street, the road where Seuss's grandparents resided. In addition, several of the characters in Seuss's stories were based upon former Springfield citizens. The author must have remembered John McGurk and August Schneelock, a real-life clerk and mailman in the town, when he created McGurk and Sneeloch's Store in *If I Ran the Circus*.

Eventually, Dr. Seuss would write more than forty-seven books, every title still in print, with more than two hundred million copies being sold. Many historical buildings and places in Springfield pay homage to Seuss's youth there; yet Springfield wanted to honor its one-time resident by creating a memorial park filled with statues depicting characters from Seuss's books.

The day I visited Springfield, I took a leisurely drive and found many images from Seuss's books in the local scenery. For example, the Howard Street Armory is a beautiful old building flanked by majestic-looking towers on either side and appears to be the inspiration for the castle in *The Five Hundred Hats of Bartholemew Cubbins*. Next, I drove to Forest Park, a place Seuss often visited as a young boy to sketch the animals he saw at the zoo located on the grounds. The ambling green of the land with its lotus ponds, footbridges, and wooded areas is reminiscent of the backdrop of *Horton Hears a Who*.

Eventually, my drive around Springfield led me to the Dr. Seuss National Memorial, located on the 140-year-old Quadrangle, which is a green stretch of land surrounded by four museums and a library, a place Seuss claimed to have "spent more time than in high school." There, I met with a committee member on the project who walked with me and described the six future statues, many of which are currently under construction in different locations and will not be unveiled until the memorial's opening this summer. My guide informed me that the statues would be the work of Lark Grey Dimond-Cates, an accomplished sculptor as well as Seuss's stepdaughter. Seuss's widow, Audrey, and former first lady Barbara Bush are honorary chairs of the six-million-dollar project.

My guide and I wandered into the whimsical Yertle Garden, which had recently been opened to the public; and I walked along a winding pathway marked with large rocks while Seussian-like pine trees stretched overhead. The soon-to-arrive Yertle the Turtle statue was described to me; sixteen-feet and ten-turtles high, it will hover over a granite reflecting pool. The park will also hold an oversized bronze chair that invites people to sit down and tell a story. Behind it will tower an open book, ten feet tall and fourteen feet wide, inscribed with text from *Oh, the Places You'll Go!* The Grinch and his dog Max peek around the corner. In another sculpture, Theodor Geisel himself will lean over his drawing board while the Cat in the Hat peers over his shoulder. All statues will be made without sharp edges to encourage child interaction, and a lighted granite pathway will lead visitors from sculpture to sculpture.

As I stood in the Quadrangle of Springfield, it seemed that both the memorial project and Dr. Seuss had accomplished their goals of providing a world of fanciful creatures that inspire children's imaginations as well as their interest in books. I thought back on my day, which included watching children play a game of make-believe and seeing a young mother reading *Horton Hatches the Egg* to her daughter in Forest Park. Just then a group of ten-year-olds sauntered into the nearby library. I thought of all the Dr. Seuss books I've enjoyed in my life and the many other books I was encouraged to read through those wonderful first experiences with *Green Eggs and Ham*. In the green landscape of the Quadrangle and within the city of Springfield, Dr. Seuss's memory and wishes live on.

Thidwick the Bighearted Moose and The Cat in the Hat will soon have places of honor in the Dr. Seuss National Memorial in Springfield, Massachusetts. Images courtesy Springfield Library and Museums Association.

FOR THE CHILDREN

Some Things Don't Make Any Sense at All

Judith Viorst

My mom says I'm her sugarplum.
My mom says I'm her lamb.
My mom says I'm completely perfect
Just the way I am.
My mom says I'm a super-special
    wonderful terrific little guy.
My mom just had another baby.
Why?

A new big brother shares a secret with his sister in OUR LITTLE
WORLD, *an original oil painting by artist Donald Zolan.
Copyright © Zolan Fine Arts, LLC, Ridgefield, Connecticut.*

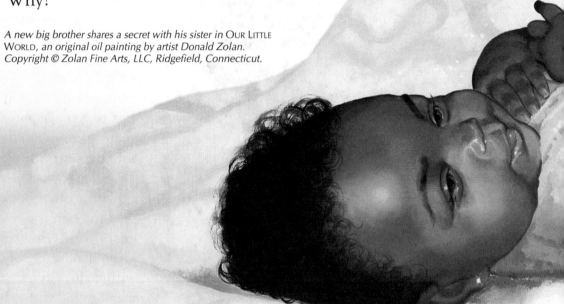

To Kim

Helen Gottschalk

Little boy, standing square,
The sun and the wind in your hair,
Heaven in your eyes, but of earth a part,
For in two grubby hands you held my heart.

Shoes on wrong, pants reversed,
Speech—original and unrehearsed.
Singing happiness in every motion,
Object of my complete devotion.

Ruler for a moment of this earthly place,
Then passing beyond all time and space.
One with the night wind, the morning star,
Heaven and my heart are where you are.

Little Girl

Lucille McBroom Crumley

My little girl, may there
Never come an hour
You can pass, indifferent to,
A first spring flower,

Or miss the magic music
Of a gentle little bird,
To linger for a lifetime
Long after it is heard,

Or the mystery of starshine
With its everlasting light
To hold you captive in its spell
On some far starless night.

My little girl, may there
Never ever come a day
You do not have the eyes to see
All beauty on your way.

PUPPETS

Laurie Hunter

I can't remember a time when I did not love puppets and enjoy viewing the world through their hand-painted eyes and stepping into their scenes of make-believe. My childhood playthings included several puppets my grandmother and mother had made for me and my sisters, including one puppet that changed from Little Red Riding Hood to Grandma with a flip of her skirt, and again to the Big Bad Wolf with a back-flip of Grandma's night cap.

I take my own children to the library every month for a marionette show, going as much for myself as for them. I also gather them around the television for an eagerly anticipated annual viewing of the von Trapp family's marionette performance in *The Sound of Music.*

So when a girlfriend of mine, Kate, invited us for a backstage tour of the puppeteer company she owns, we greedily accepted the invitation. We stepped back in surprise when Kate led us behind the showy velvet curtains. Rows and rows of characters dangled limply from wooden pegs on the wall while mounds of stage props littered the expanse of floor. Kate cordially introduced us, one by one, to her entire personal collection of rare and one-of-a-kind puppets and marionettes.

As my wide-eyed children watched, Kate shared one of her worn, well-loved, and weathered puppets. Most of her puppets have seen years of use, but their balding hair or scuffed faces only seem to add to their magical beauty.

Kate's favorite marionette, which can be better termed a work of art, is a porcelain fairy-tale princess, and I gawked at its intricate gown as Kate described each detail. Patterned after eighteenth-century dress styles, the marionette's skirts were drawn up in the back like curtains, revealing remarkably tiny shoes that can lightly tiptoe across the stage. Real human hair is scalloped into miniature braids that peek out from underneath her plumed bonnet. Her mouth is her best feature—a tiny red dot which seems to pout or smile or laugh when Kate jerks the marionette strings into lifelike nods and glances.

Kate's other puppets we met included a green caterpillar that must be manipulated by three puppeteers at once, a winged unicorn, an Arabian dancer, a formidable troop of jointed wooden soldiers, and many more. Her collection also included puppets made from papier-maché, resin, clay, and cloth to resemble such fantastic creatures as a fire-breathing dragon (smoke-like mist is puffed realistically out of his mouth), a pair of Tweedle-Dee Tweedle-Dum puppets hinged together like Siamese twins, and a bird with turquoise feathers sprouting from the top of her head. Every animal imaginable was represented in Kate's collection; a menagerie of flat shadow puppets were made to travel two by two on little wooden rods toward a massive cardboard ark.

Kate learned to puppeteer in the drama club in college. Her interest grew from there as she began to make her own puppets and marionettes by hand to stock the college's sparse choices. Not wanting to leave her new hobby at graduation, she launched her own puppeteer company. She frequently adds to her collection, spending anywhere from three hundred to three thousand dollars for each new addition. She trains each puppeteer herself, clearly conveying the importance of treating the puppets as if they too were members of the staff.

As my children and I regretfully headed for the backstage exit door, I took one last look at Kate's family of puppets. A unique opportunity immediately came to mind. I remembered where my Little Red Riding Hood puppet was stored and decided to unearth it for my children to enjoy. A puppet really has no business being packed away for a rare performance. Its magic lies in its ability to turn an ordinary day into an imaginative one and to spring to life, if only for an hour or two.

Not Just Child's Play

If you would like to collect puppets, the following information may be helpful.

The History of Puppets

• Puppets have been enjoyed for thousands of years, the first ones most likely being string-operated, jointed dolls used in religious ceremonies to help teach and amaze audiences.

• The earliest mention of puppets can be found in "Mahabharata," an ancient Indian poem written in the ninth century.

• Today, some form of puppetry can be found in almost every country.

Types of Puppets

• Hand—This type usually has a cloth body and hollow head that fits over and is moved by the hand of the puppeteer.

• Finger—This form, the simplest, is operated by a single finger.

• Marionettes—These typically wooden figures with jointed limbs are moved from above by attached strings or wires. Each string is connected to a different part of the puppet. Marionettes may have merely three or four well-placed strings or more than one hundred!

• Rod—Traditionally found in Japanese theater, this variety of puppet is usually operated by rods from below by puppeteers who are dressed in black and working in full view of the audience.

• Shadow—A shadow puppet is operated against a thin silk screen and backlit by strong light. The audience sees only the shadows.

• Dummy—This puppet figure is operated by a ventriloquist, who throws his voice so that the dummy appears to be speaking.

• Wayang Kulit—In Indonesia, these leather shadow puppets are used to present plays based on Hindu myths.

• Wayang Golek—These Indonesian rod puppets, which date back to A.D. 100, are operated by a central rod that controls the head with additional rods connected to the hands.

Tips for Collecting

• Narrow your collection to one type of puppet

A group of collectible puppets in Madrid, Spain, awaits their next adventure. Photo by Jessie Walker.

once you've defined your favorite.

• Seek handmade varieties rather than those turned out by factories.

• Try collecting a set of puppets that work together to tell a complete story.

• You may also want to try your hand at making your own puppets for your collection. This heirloom craft is often taught at craft shops, art supply stores, public libraries, and local theaters.

Maintaining Your Collection

• Dust puppets to clean them rather than washing with water. Many paints, glues, and top coats are water soluble.

• Avoid light. Over time, bright light will damage your puppets. Resist the urge to showcase valuable pieces of your collection in glass cases or cabinets. For long-term storage, use the puppets' original boxes or store in cushioned suitcases.

• Make sure all packaging for storage is acid-free.

• Deter threats from moths and woodworms by keeping an insecticide in your storage container. (Moth balls can leave a permanent smell.)

• Avoid moisture and heat.

Lovely Things

Grace V. Watkins

A little girl's soft-whispered prayer
Is lovelier than any fair
Andante wind through country air.

A small boy's worship-shining face
Has more of loveliness and grace
Than any sea's noon-golden space.

Who helps a child to find the light
Of faith has done a deed more bright
Than all the stars within the night!

Humble Parent

Gail Brook Burket

"My Child," I say with pride. But I am wrong.
A child is the sum total of all things
He has experienced and each day brings
More understanding as he grasps the long
Magnificence of time and space, the strong
Dependability of earth. Life sings
New melodies of sun and shining wings
Each day for him in never ending song.

The many teachers who have loved and taught
This child have left an imprint clearly seen
In attitudes and ardors he has caught.
The church has given him her own serene
Assurance of man's worth. I have but brought
Him to the golden fields where he can glean.

A mother waits for her tiny helper in A Sunny Morning, Villiers-Le-Bel *by artist Frederick Childe Hassam. Image from Christie's Images.*

A SLICE OF LIFE

Douglas Malloch

Art by Eve DeGrie

HE'S GOT A GIRL

We used to think, his ma and me,
How sort of jealous we would be
When Sonny got along to where
He had a girl—and now he's there.
He never noticed them till now;
And yet we knew sometime, somehow,
A laughing eye, a golden curl
Would set his boyish heart awhirl,
And then we'd know he had a girl.

Oh, yes, she might be sweet and good
As any youngster ever could;
We ain't a bit afraid of that,
And that ain't what I'm driving at.
But even in the second grade
We always felt a bit afraid;
We always felt afraid because
We feared, like other mas and pas,
He wouldn't be the boy he was.

And now it's happened—certain as
The signs of spring—we know it has.
For now he parts and combs his hair
And asks for something clean to wear,
And trims his nails, and ties his tie,
And shines his shoes—and we know why.
When any boy unasked appears
To wash his neck behind the ears,
That's love—no matter what his years.

He's got a girl. And me, his dad,
And Ma, we both are rather glad.
We thought we'd hate to have our son
To ever care for anyone
Excepting us; but, dear me suz,
As Mother says, we're glad he does.
No jealous thoughts our hearts annoy,
In fact it's added to our joy:
My, how it has improved that boy!

To My Child

Gail Brook Burket

My youth flew like a swallow's wings at dawn.
I did not see it go nor realize
Those fleeting years of joy were wholly gone,
Because I saw the world through your young eyes.
I shared the warm enthusiastic glow
Of childhood and your first clear glimpse of God.
When school days came, I watched you proudly go
That shining day of sun and goldenrod.
You found a world which grew apace each day.
I helped you build high castles in the air
And shared the hurts and triumphs on your way.
Although the years have silver tinged my hair
And etched upon my face a tale well told,
Your youth has kept my heart from growing old.

My Gift to You

Ada Flanders

My dear, I will not give you worldly things.
To you I send a song when my heart sings,
To you, the ever-changing sunset's glow,
The early dawn reflected on the snow,
The scent of lilacs drenched with summer rain,
The fairy snowflakes on your windowpane,
A cozy nook to listen to the wind
And watch the shadows dance undisciplined,
A hearth fire when the nights are long and cold
To dream by embers' glow of castles old;
A path by river's bend to roam at will,
A place to talk to God on windswept hill.
My dear, these things on you I would bestow;
I sing this song that I may tell you so.

Nature is shared in MOTHER AND CHILD IN PINE WOODS *by artist
Edmund Charles Tarbell. Image from Christie's Images.*

Devotions FROM THE Heart

Pamela Kennedy

The aged women likewise, that they be in behavior as becometh holiness, not false accusers, not given to much wine, teachers of good things. Titus 2:3

THE BLESSING OF AUNTIES

We had just moved into our new home in Hawaii a few years ago, and we were outside doing some yard work. A fellow from down the street walked by with his three-year-old daughter and stopped to chat, welcoming us to the neighborhood. His little girl was carrying a plumeria blossom she had plucked from a low branch, and as they got ready to continue their walk, the father said, "Give the auntie your flower, Kara. Tell her 'aloha.'" Dutifully, the little girl looked up at me with sparkling eyes, smiled, and handed me her flower. I tucked it behind my ear as she threw a kiss and walked on with her daddy.

That was my introduction to the Hawaiian concept of "auntie." Unlike other places in our country where the term is limited to those female relatives who happen to be siblings of your parents, in Hawaii an auntie can be any older woman for whom one holds affection. At the school where I teach, the woman who comes to teach our students the dances and chants of the ancient Hawaiians is known by everyone as Auntie Ala. In our church, there are many aunties who regularly scold, hug, cajole, teach, encourage, and comfort younger people. It makes no difference if you have no nearby kin; if you're a young person in Hawaii, there is never a lack of aunties to talk to or take you places, to watch you perform in your school play, or to cheer you on in a soccer game. And often, young adults seek out their aunties for advice or comfort, for a sympathetic ear, or just for a fun time. It's an informal network of caring that crosses boundaries

> Dear Father, help me to recognize young people who might need comforting and encouragement. Let me be a woman who lives as an example of Your love in my world.

of race, family, economics, and generations.

I think this might have been what Paul was thinking about when he encouraged Titus, a young pastor in ancient Crete. Along with all the other advice he parceled out about church policy and doctrine, Paul recognized the importance of keeping a community together by mutual care and concern. He saw the value of having the older and more mature women encourage the younger ones by not only modeling wise lifestyle choices but by passing on the good things about their culture and traditions. He affirmed the value of women helping women. In a sense, he might have said, "Be an auntie!"

Reaching out to others with personal, loving concern has never been more needed. Many of us live in isolation, separated by high-rise buildings, busy schedules, too many commitments, and too much technology. We have substituted e-mails for hand-written notes, phone calls for conversations, and digital photo albums for face-to-face visits. Perhaps what we need to develop is a generation of aunties that is willing to share their lives with younger people. Despite all our modern conveniences, nothing has been invented to replace the lap, the hug, a hand to hold, or a sympathetic shoulder to lean on. As we age, we have a treasury of experiences and stories to share—and perhaps even a bit more time. What might happen if we looked for opportunities to illustrate Paul's words to Titus and became women who live as examples of truth and holiness, teaching good things? What if we all became aunties?

The artist's own childhood image with her grandmother is pictured in RADIANT SPAN, © copyright Deidre Scherer, 1997. Fabric and thread medium, twenty-eight by twenty-five inches. From the artist's book DEIDRE SCHERER: WORK IN FABRIC AND THREAD (C & T Publishing, 1998).

Grandmother's Tapestry

Vera L. Seter

Throughout the years you've made no claim
To artistry; yet clear and fine
You've fashioned with your patient hands
A tapestry of rare design.

'Twas not with riches that you wove,
But chose for threads of precious gold
A childish kiss, a baby's smile,
Brave songs and dreams to clasp and hold.

Guardian

Vachel Lindsay

The moon is but a candleglow
That flickers thro' the gloom;
The starry space, a castle hall;
And Earth, the children's room,
Where all night long the old trees stand
To watch the streams asleep:
Grandmothers guarding trundle beds,
Good shepherds guarding sheep.

The Mothers of the Earth

Grace Noll Crowell

The woman who has borne a child,
We pause to honor her today;
The woman who has led a child
With patience down life's broad highway;
The woman who has God's own heart,
His tenderness and gentle grace,
Who comes to Him for needed strength,
Who meets Him daily face to face.

The woman who a thousand times
Would bear her agony of pain
To save her child from needless hurt;
To keep him clean and free from stain;
To know that he would walk at last
A man across the world's bright sod,
An honor to his land, his flag;
A glory to his home, his God.

The woman who has borne a child—
No one may choose a better part.
The woman who is kind and wise,
Who moves with quiet mind and heart,
Whose love surrounds a little child
To meet his daily, constant need,
Who spends her life that he may live—
We honor her today indeed.

Three generations show their love in MOTHER LOVE by artist Ferdinand Georg Waldmuller. Image from Superstock.

A Tribute to Grandmother

Mildred Maralyn Mercer

All that I can give to life will be
To hold a crimson sunset in the sky,
Or catch a birdsong as it flutters by,
Or string the stars on moonbeams that I see.
While all the things that you have done for me—
And all the rest who often wonder why
You do so much and how your hands can fly
Will be an unforgotten melody.

My poems and songs can only be the leaves.
Your life has been the tree.

My Song

Ramona Vernon

I sing of you because your long
And busy days are gladly spent
In loving tasks, while your content
Spreads through our home like joyful song.

You quiet fear with tenderness;
Your laughter breaks the twilight gloom
Until sleep fills a moonlit room
And beholds the peace of your caress.

Oh, gratefully my glad heart sings
A song of simple, happy days,
A grandmother's understanding ways
And love that lives in little things.

Grandmother's treasures tell of a lifetime of memories. Photo by Jessie Walker.

Bits
and
Pieces

*P*ity the child who's never known a
grandmother he could call his own.

—*Author Unknown*

*C*hildren do not realize how deep is
grandmother love, how wise.

—*Author Unknown*

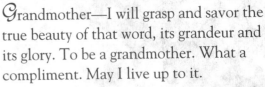

*G*randmother—I will grasp and savor the
true beauty of that word, its grandeur and
its glory. To be a grandmother. What a
compliment. May I live up to it.

—*Marjorie Holmes*

*G*randmothers are to life what the Ph.D. is to
education. There is nothing you can feel, taste,
expect, predict, or want that the grandmothers
in your family do not know about in detail.

—*Lois Wyse*

A happy youth, and their old age is beautiful and free.

—*William Wordsworth*

*F*or age is opportunity no less
Than youth itself, though in another dress.

—*Henry Wadsworth Longfellow*

*B*lessed be the hand that prepares a
pleasure for a child, for there is no say-
ing when and where it may bloom forth.

—*Douglas Jerrold*

I have often thought what a melancholy
world this would be without children; and
what an inhuman world without the aged.

—*Samuel Taylor Coleridge*

*L*oving, thoughtful, imaginative
grandparents really live in the
hearts of their grandchildren.

—*Elva Anson*

The Eye of the Beholder

Anne Campbell

When Grandpa looks at Grandma,
Somehow he doesn't see
Her wrinkled brow; her hair, white now;
Her aged serenity.
He doesn't see her falter
When night its darkness brings.
That she is slow he'll never know—
Or any of those things!

When Grandpa looks at Grandma,
Somehow he doesn't hear
The broken tones that now she owns;
Her voice seems firm and clear.
Her eyes that smile upon him
Are faded blue and dim.
Though time has ranged, they have not changed;
They look the same to him.

When Grandpa looks at Grandma,
Forgetting she is old,
He sees his bride cling to his side
With hair of shining gold.
He sees her in the splendor. Love just grows and grows.
If she is gray and bent today,
Grandfather never knows!

Concerning Fruitcake

Grace V. Watkins

Grandmother cut off a slice for me,
And then with a twinkle she said,
"It was made a long, long time ago, child,
The week before I was wed.
Everyone knows
That fruitcake is sweeter the older it grows."

Grandfather winked from his chair. Said he,
"With the dictum on fruitcake I fully agree.
The same is true
Of grandmothers too."

Their smiles say it all in THE HAPPY COUPLE *by artist Luigi Bechi.
Image from Christie's Images.*

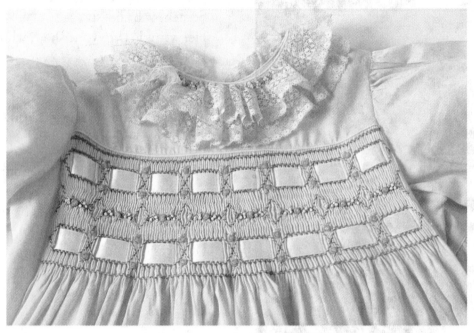

Delicate smocking adorns a dress. Used with permission of Sterling Publishing Co., Inc. from CREATIVE SMOCKING by Chris Rankin, copyright © 1997 by Lark Books. Photo by Evan Bracken.

SMOCKING

Lisa Ragan

My grandmother was of an era gone by, an era where girls learned to sew before they finished grade school and then grew up making everything from bed linens to wedding gowns themselves. My mother, on the other hand, never even learned to sew, not having any need with an abundance of affordable, ready-to-wear dresses available. As for my generation, a home-sewn garment has become increasingly rare in our busy, bustling lives. Nonetheless, this year I yearned to make something special in honor of Mother's Day, in honor of the generations of women who have gone before me. Since my cousin and his wife recently welcomed a baby girl to their family, I decided to revive a technique I'd seen my grandmother employ and create an old-fashioned smocked baby dress as a gift for little Madeleine.

At its most basic, smocking is the application of decorative stitches on pleated material. Traditional English smocking has been worked on clothing for more than three hundred years. The style began as a

way to control the fullness of material and provide more comfortable movement for the wearer. The word *smocking* comes from *smock*, also called a shift, which was a garment comprised of simple rectangles of fabric with smocking on the front and back that allowed for easy movement. One of the earliest known references to a smock appears in 1386 in "The Miller's Tale," wherein Chaucer writes of a smock-wearing woman. The history of smocking can also be traced through artwork, such as the smocking on the Virgin Mary's dress in Hans Memling's *The Rest on the Flight into Egypt* (1465).

By the late fifteenth century, loose-fitting smocks were common garments for both men and women, with the peasant class wearing smocks as outer garments and the more wealthy Europeans wearing smocks as undergarments. The smock, or chemise, worn under a lady's gown was usually of a richly embroidered white linen that fell well below the calf. So beautiful was the smocking on the undergarment that the outer dress was often cut low and the sleeves slit to reveal the embroidered chemise underneath.

The popularity of the smock continued to grow throughout the centuries and reached its peak by the 1800s. Although the simple smock itself soon passed out of fashion altogether, the technique of smocking remained popular in women's and children's clothing. By the Victorian era, women often wore silk dresses embellished with elaborate smocking.

Smocking in the United States has been taught to young women for generations, dating from the time of the first colonial wives who smocked work clothing for their farming husbands. With the invention of elastic, smocking was no longer needed to control fullness in garments. And whereas smocking has not again enjoyed the height of popularity as it did in seventeenth- and eighteenth-century England, the technique has survived through the ages. Today, one can find smocking books and magazines, classes, and an abundance of patterns and techniques as well as innovative projects, such as purses and lampshades.

I was pleased to learn that smocking is a great technique for a beginning needleworker since it requires only basic sewing skills and no special tools. Virtually any fabric that drapes well can be smocked. Because it can be difficult to estimate the width of fabric needed for gathering, experts recommend smocking a small sample of the fabric first to get an idea of the thickness of the fabric, the type of stitch used (a cable stitch is tighter than honeycomb, for example), tension level, and distance between gathers. Fabric lengths of anywhere from two to six times the width of the area to be smocked are common. Washable fabrics should be washed before smocking.

Through the years, smockers have invented an impressive number of ways to pleat the fabric area that will be smocked. Some beginning needleworkers choose to have their fabric pleated by machine at a sewing supply store for a nominal fee. Most of the other options consist of various ways to apply dots to the fabric and then gather the fabric together by connecting the dots. These options include using graph paper, tissue paper, a template, a pencil and ruler, or iron-on transfers. Additional gathering methods include counting threads, using a mechanical pleater, or simply judging the distance between pleats by eye. Some needleworkers recommend that beginning smockers select a patterned fabric such as gingham or dotted Swiss and then use the pattern itself as a guide for gathering.

Just as most any fabric can be selected for a smocking project, most any thread can be used for the smocking stitches. The thread used to pull the gathers together needs to be strong enough that it will not break. As for the smocking thread, many smockers choose three strands of embroidery floss. Thread choices also include cotton, silk, metallic, yarn, or even fine silk ribbon. Some smocking designs call for more than one color of smocking thread to give the finished piece an additional dimensional effect. As for needles, expert smockers recommend using a sharp crewel needle (available in varying sizes), although a chenille needle can be used when smocking coarse fabrics or using thicker threads.

Smocking stitches are essentially the same as those used in embroidery but feel different because they are used on pleats. The needleworker must adjust the tension of the stitches in order to accommodate the pleats. The best smockers make a sampler before each project so they can test certain stitches on different fabrics. Smocking stitches include the bullion stitch, bullion roses, cable stitch, chain stitch, honeycomb stitch, chevron stitch (also called diamond stitch), dimensional stitch, French knot, herringbone, satin stitch, lazy daisy stitch, outline stitch, stem stitch, trellis stitch (also called wave stitch), and the vandyke stitch. Although the list of stitches that can be used in smocking can be overwhelming to a beginner, some of the most beautiful pieces use only one stitch, such as honeycomb.

Some smocking designs feature pictures of animals, fruits, vegetables, flowers, or other objects. These picture designs and some of the looser geometric designs require that the needleworker backsmock the piece. Backsmocking, usually achieved with a cable stitch that will not show in the front, holds the gathers firmly in place so that the front smocking can be freer in design.

Even though I did not grow up learning to sew as a necessity, I truly enjoy building my skills in the needle arts of my grandmother's generation. I hope that little Madeleine's smocked baby dress, hand-stitched with delicate embroidery, becomes a treasured heirloom for my cousin's family. And if Madeleine is so inclined, perhaps someday I can teach her the centuries-old technique of smocking.

Infant Granddaughter
(Thoughts at two A.M.)
Harriet Whipple

I looked upon this miracle
With gratitude and pride
As she snuggled on my shoulder,
Replete and satisfied.
Warm and heavy there upon me,
Eyes closed so very tight;
We breathed as one together
In the quiet of the night.
She felt so much a part of me
As her mother had before;
Her baby trust and helplessness
Made me but love her more.
I felt such a closeness to her—
A continuity
From generations that are past
To those still yet to be.
My cheek caressed her downy hair;
I held her tiny hand
With a tenderness and wonder
Only mothers understand.

Left: A few of Mother and Baby's favorite things are gathered in this photo by Jessie Walker. Above: Grandmother cherishes every moment with the newest generation. Photo by Camille Tokerud/International Stock.

Grandbaby
Elizabeth B. Estes

Sometimes, dear child, I forget
The exact expression
In your inquisitive brown eyes.
Other times I can't recall
The contour of your cherub-cheeks.
What precisely do your hands
Look like—and your feet?
But my arms, like the collective
Memory of every woman
Who has held a cherished child,
Know the weight, the warmth,
The feel, the love of holding you.
Always, a woman's arms remember.

THROUGH MY WINDOW

Pamela Kennedy

Art by Meredith Johnson

EMPTY NESTING

I anticipated it like the plague. All through my daughter's senior year, just thinking about having a house bereft of offspring caused my eyes to fill with tears. My husband didn't get it. He said comforting things like, "You won't have to do after-school pickups. You'll have more time to yourself. Meals will be simpler, quicker, easier." He didn't understand that I liked picking our daughter up from school and hearing about her day. I didn't want more time to myself. And cooking for two is often much harder than doing it for three!

I tried to explain it to him. "Imagine you're doing a job you really love, and you've done a pretty good job of it for about twenty-six years. And then someone says, 'Hey, guess what. You're retired now.' But you don't want to retire."

He had an answer for that too. "Just get another job! Go out and do something you've been wanting to do but didn't have time for."

I replied that I wanted to keep being a mom. He sighed and gave me that "what am I going to do with you" look. Then he hugged me and said, "Hey, you'll still be a mom, just in a different way." Somehow I didn't feel very reassured.

Time, as it has a tendency to do, marched on, and we went through graduation and summer vacation. All too soon it was time for college orientation. Because of the high cost of shipping from Hawaii and the limited sources for "mainland winter supplies," my daughter and I flew to Seattle a week early so we could accumulate bedding and warm clothes and other necessities for her dorm room. We had a marvelous time buying sweaters and coats and heavy shoes, comforters, jeans, and flannel sheets. We laughed and talked about all kinds of things; and when we called home to report on our progress, I happily informed my husband that all this pre-college shopping was helping to take the sting out of preparing for the empty nest. He groaned. I reminded him that it was his suggestion to go out and do something I hadn't had time for before!

"Yes, but . . ."

"I'll call you soon; we have to get to the linen outlet before it closes." I hung up and gave my daughter a thumbs-up sign.

Moving-in day finally came, and there were so many things to be done that we hardly had time to think. Three college girls settling into a twelve-foot-by-nineteen-foot room doesn't leave much time for sorrow or reflection. As the orientation weekend progressed, we were busy moving from one meeting to another, attending picnics, and listening to speakers. The reality that my last child, and only daughter, would not be returning home with me in a few days began to sink in. I was happy for her, excited about the wonderful opportunities, eager for her to try her wings and realize that she really did know how to fly. But in the back of my mind, I wondered about my own capacity to return to the nest alone.

The time came for good-byes, and we shed a few tears together over a cup of herb tea. Then she walked with me to the car and we embraced. "Oh, Mom," she sobbed.

"I know," was all I could whisper. It was a

> *The reality that my last child would not be returning home with me in a few days began to sink in. I was eager for her to try her wings. . . . but I wondered about my own capacity to return to the nest alone.*

change, a rite of passage; and I knew things wouldn't be the same when I saw her again in several months. Suddenly I remembered a ritual she had when she was in elementary school. We lived in a house on a corner, and every morning when she left the house she would walk across the street and pass a high laurel hedge. Just before she turned the corner and went around the hedge, she'd look back at me and wave. She called it her "magic corner." She said it was because after she turned the corner, everything from the morning disappeared and the whole new day spread out ahead of her, just waiting to be discovered.

"Annie," I whispered. "Look over there." Across the parking lot, a flight of broad, red brick steps marched up the hillside between plantings of geraniums and a laurel hedge. "It's your magic corner. You walk across there and start up the stairs, and just before you turn the corner, look back. I'll be standing right here waving." We hugged once more, and I kissed her; then she walked away. I watched her as she slowly started up the steps, then caught my breath as she turned and waved. She looked so much like that little girl in third grade, and yet she stood with a confidence and courage that I knew would guide her well.

I raised my arm and waved bravely in return. It was a farewell that I had not wanted to happen, but it was also a wave of hello. Ahead of each of us lay a bright new day, waiting to be discovered. Like it or not, we were both moving into new territory. She would be learning to fly, and I would be learning how to rearrange my nest to accommodate two once more. Somehow, despite my tears, I had a sense of peace that we would both be just fine.

Pamela Kennedy is a freelance writer of short stories, articles, essays, and children's books. Wife of a retired naval officer and mother of three children, she has made her home on both U.S. coasts and currently resides in Honolulu, Hawaii.

Some Simple Thing

Anona McConaghy

The happenings of my childhood seem
A misty half-remembered dream,
Almost obscured by added tiers
Memory builds through the years
Until some simple, common thing
Releases them. With feral spring
They leap to life, full-bodied, bright,
As if occurring yesternight;
Some sound or taste or fragrancy
Returns the child I used to be.

Going Home

Vera Dolores Bromley

Going home—care slips away
And I am back to yesterday
Where love and peace and tranquil hours
Bloom once again among the flowers.

All of the values that really last
Are here where I left them in the past
To show me again that love is king,
And a home where it dwells is everything.

In the Shadows of an Attic

Edith Helstern

In the shadows of an attic when the morning sun is high,
Peeping through an eastern window from out a clear blue sky,
The past and present mingle with the memories in my heart
As I stand and gaze at treasures stored, forgotten for a part.

Guilt-edged picture frames and what-nots and a quaint old cherry clock,
And a marble-top old dresser, built of good old-fashioned stock.
Grandma's huge, outdated birdcage hangs upon the ceiling wall,
And the old lamp-lighter's lantern sits in readiness for call.

Lampshades, hatracks, and old cushions, magazines and posters rare
Share a shelf with dusty treasures at the top of those old stairs.
And I dust the old worn rocker that was once my mother's pride,
And I sit and gently ponder through the tears I cannot hide.

An attic holds a lifetime of childhood fun. Photo by Dianne Dietrich Leis/Dietrich Stock Photo, Inc.

One Child's Music

Carol Hogan

To one small child, music
Is as natural as daylight.
It's the sound of grasshopper knees
Rubbing together, honeybees
Motoring from flower to flower,
Fluttering wings in a maple,
The whippoorwill's call in the evening.

To the listening child, music
Is blackberries and red currants
Shimmering among green leaves.
It is acorns quietly dropping
And Queen Anne's lace shaping umbrellas.
It is dew drops wiggling in webs
And the silk of milkweed drifting,
The essence of pennyroyal
Sweating a summer perfume,
And the yellow centers of daisies
Squeezed in the palm to promise
The number of her children.

It's a loving grandmother singing
Hymns as she hangs out washes
Or rolls new peas from their pods,
Counterpoint and staccato,
Into a metal pot.
It's sitting on her lap and finding
Poems of love in her eyes.

To the small child, the world is music,
Small symphonies of music
As warm as the sun and as free,
As unrehearsed as she is.

A mother and toddler share the joys of a spring day in this photo by Daniel Dempster.

The Good, the Gentle

Author Unknown

The grass grows slowly up the hill
With faith the torrent cannot kill,
And rocks are rough, and still the clover
The stony fields will yet run over—
And I know nothing that the true,
The good, the gentle cannot do.

Woodlands that the winters sadden
The leaves of spring again will gladden;
And so must life forever be—
The gentle hands work patiently
And yet accomplish more forever
Than these too strong or those too clever.

So toils an undiscouraged God
And covers barren fields with sod,
And so will hate and sin surrender
To faith still strong and love still tender—
And I know nothing that the true,
The good, the gentle cannot do.

True goodness is like the glowworm in this, that it shines most when no eyes, except those of heaven, are upon it.

—J. C. and A. W. Hare

Brilliant spring phlox cascades over a hillside in Lemington, Vermont. Photo by William H. Johnson/Johnson's Photography.

When Lilacs Bloom

Isla Paschal Richardson

The very word *lilacs* has fragrance, song,
And poetry. A world of fairyland,
Childhood's enchantment to these shrubs belong.

Oh, they should not be placed in gardens planned
And formal, but in careless clusters grow
Where little children play and birdbaths stand.

Lilacs love homes and with a tranquil glow
Exude serenity as if to bless
The humans they have learned to know.

Against time's dull demands and sharp duress,
In memory these arborescent flowers
Bring flashes of recurrent tenderness

With springtime's magic breath of their perfume;
And we are young again—when lilacs bloom.

The Old Lilac Bush

Osman Castle Hooper

There's a lovely spot that memory knows
Where a sweet-breathed lilac ever grows;
The bush grows strong, and its blooms contain
The sweets distilled by sun and rain.

It grew and flowered there years ago;
And in wondrous ways that the fairies know,
It gathered the sweets from day to day
To throw at the feet of radiant May.

I saw the old lilac bush today
As it stood arrayed in its own fair way;
Like clustered grapes hung the fragrant flower,
And I felt the thrill of a long-gone hour.

Oh, sweet is the fragrance, lilac fair,
That you offer free to the grateful air,
But dearer than perfume, bloom and all,
Are the memories fond your sweets recall.

A rustic bench in East Arlington, Vermont, offers a view of both flower and stream. Photo by William H. Johnson/Johnson's Photography.

Small Offerings

Kim Konopka

In my overgrown garden, I weed,
Trying to untangle a season of neglect.
Across the yard, from an old hose,
My daughter collects water into
Cupped hands and slowly
Walks the offering toward me.
The liquid dribbles between soft fingers,
Sprinkles small bare feet.

She arrives, arms stretched high,
Then sees she has nothing to give me.
My gloved finger points to her toes,
Glistening with the lost drops,
And tears begin to form.
Leaning down, I bring her hands
To my lips and swallow all
Her empty drink and whisper,
    pretend water is so much sweeter.

A young girl tries her hand at gardening. Photo by Joe Willis/International Stock.

His First Garden

Erica May Brooks

Whoever you are,
Pause before you go your way
And tread with care;
For this is a sacred spot.
This plot is the garden of a tiny tot.

Whoever you are,
Remember it, as you go your way.
If you have time to spare,
Add a prayer tonight
That the gayest flowers may bloom
For his delight.

A toddler plants the summer's future harvest. Photo by Joe Willis/International Stock.

Readers' Reflections

Editor's Note: Readers are invited to submit original poetry for possible publication in future issues of Ideals. Please send typed copies only; manuscripts will not be returned. Writers receive $10 for each published submission. Send material to Readers' Reflections, Ideals Publications, 535 Metroplex Drive, Suite 250, Nashville, Tennessee 37211.

Mother's Day Treat
G. L. Heuer
Belvidere, Illinois

I saw a robin's nest today
On a tree limb just so high
With blue eggs the color of a summer sky.
Mama robin waited for me to go away
Then settled in the nest for the day.
Papa robin was never too far away.

Soon there will be baby birds to feed.
Mama and Papa will seek for
Food to fill their need.
They will grow bigger, and soon
Feathers will show.
Mama and Papa will teach them as they grow.
Time will come when they all will go,
And that will be the end of my show.

All there will be left is an empty nest
On a tree limb just so high
Under summer's sun and clear blue sky.

A Small Bouquet
Grant K. Davis
Otterbein, Indiana

She knelt down among the blades of grass
To pick a small bouquet,
To give it to her mother
On a very special day.
First she picked some dandelions
With blooms of yellow bright
Then looked around for something else
To make a pretty sight.
So then she picked some violets,
The ones of purple hue,
But thought she needed something else
Before her job was through.
Then she picked some blades of grass
And placed them one by one
Then leaned back to take a look,
So proud of what she'd done.
So back into the house she ran,
Her mother to surprise.
The birthday gift from this young girl
Brought tears to Mother's eyes.

Cradlesong

Diana Kwiatkowski Rubin
Piscataway, New Jersey

How sweet the smile
Of the baby in spring!
The joy he possesses,
The happiness he brings!

Take your flowers,
Fine springtime bliss!
Nothing is so lovely
As the baby's gentle kiss!

Ribbons of Flowers

Gay Sorensen
Olympia, Washington

Ribbons of flowers to tie in her hair
That framed her face, so tiny and fair,
Brought out the color of her eyes,
The softest shade of clear blue skies.

I braided her hair each morning just so
And tied each end in a colorful bow.
But when the day came that she wanted it cut,
I knew that my child was fast growing up.
Now she's a mother and grandmother too,
Yet she still has those soft, clear eyes of blue.
But the blond, braided hair tied in ribbons so gay
Is now light brown and tinged with gray.

When I see pretty ribbons, I remember those days
When she was small with the sweetest of ways.
And I still have those precious mem'ries where
I tied those ribbons in her hair.

The Flower in My Garden

Helen Olsen
East Tray, Wisconsin

You're the flower in my garden,
Rooted deep within my heart
With a love that stems gigantic
From the day you had your start
As a tiny seed that sprouted
In the latter part of May,
With outstretched petals and budding stem—
What a grand and glorious day!

I pray your delicate, blossoming stem
Can bend with wind and storm,
That gentle rains from heaven
Refresh you every morn
With radiant color and fragrance
Only full-grown flowers know
And share with those who reveled in
The chance to watch them grow.

The Gardener blessed you with a smile
Of sunshine on your face;
He gave you dew-kissed twinkling eyes,
Your special winsome grace.
I praise the Master Gardener
For this lovely work of art,
The flower in my garden
Rooted deep within my heart.

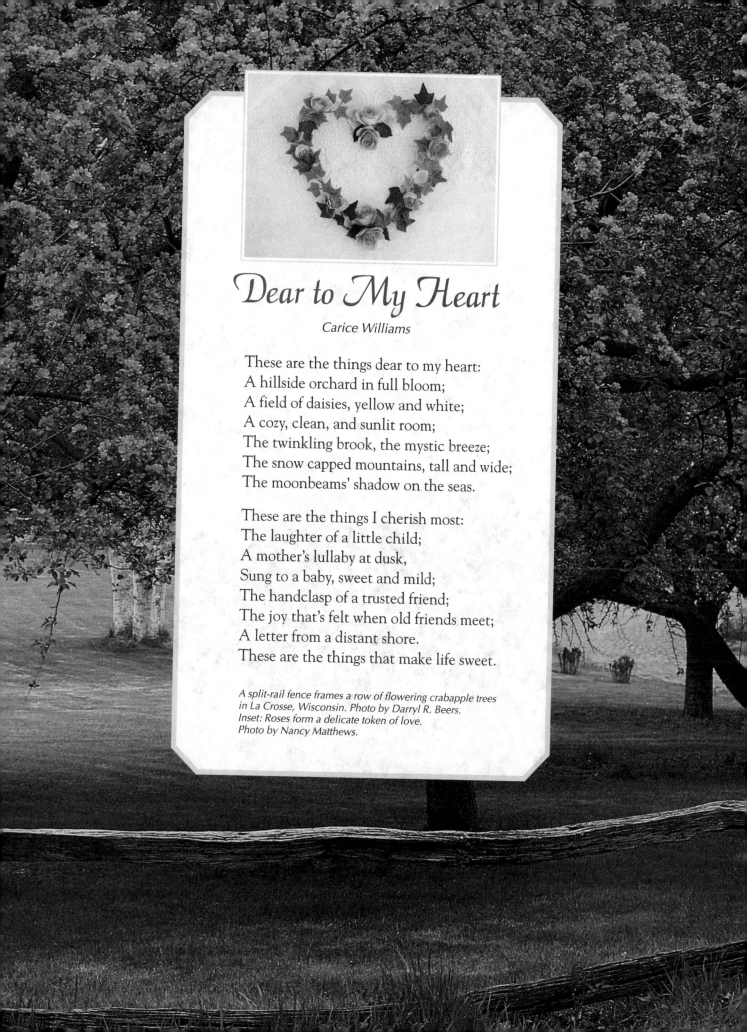

Dear to My Heart

Carice Williams

These are the things dear to my heart:
A hillside orchard in full bloom;
A field of daisies, yellow and white;
A cozy, clean, and sunlit room;
The twinkling brook, the mystic breeze;
The snow capped mountains, tall and wide;
The moonbeams' shadow on the seas.

These are the things I cherish most:
The laughter of a little child;
A mother's lullaby at dusk,
Sung to a baby, sweet and mild;
The handclasp of a trusted friend;
The joy that's felt when old friends meet;
A letter from a distant shore.
These are the things that make life sweet.

*A split-rail fence frames a row of flowering crabapple trees
in La Crosse, Wisconsin. Photo by Darryl R. Beers.
Inset: Roses form a delicate token of love.
Photo by Nancy Matthews.*

MAY TWILIGHT

How delightful the May twilight! Here from the highest hill I watch the evening come while the valley below sweeps into the shadows of the setting sun. The surface of the land seems to undulate with the changing light, and the valley slowly turns into a mystery in the contour of the slopes. The deeper shades of light penetrate the valleylands while the higher hills still feel the brightness of the sun's soft lingering rays.

The nearby creek winds down the hills; I listen to its song. The buildings in the valley are graceful forms etched into the fading light. How small they seem from far away, and how small the towering trees as they sink into the deepening darkness.

I think of the valley as preparing for the night. Birds retire to the trees and hedges. Night stills their songs, except for the organ roll of the thrush from the woods nearby.

A misty dampness grows heavy upon leaf and grass and bloom. Night is closing the doors of the day, and the shades are being drawn.

A final surge of light spreads a faint halo on the highest hill as I turn my steps toward the valley, now a lake of darkness far below. I picture myself as a swimmer, stroking my way toward an island of light, a house where the glowing streams of light pour out from the windows into the quietness of night.

The author of three books, Lansing Christman has contributed to Ideals for almost thirty years. Mr. Christman has also been published in several American, foreign, and braille anthologies. He lives in rural South Carolina.

The moonrise and mist fill the Newfound River Valley in New Hampshire. Photo by William H. Johnson/Johnson's Photography.

Beyond the Garden Gate

Nora M. Bozeman

Beyond the garden gate I see
A graceful weeping willow tree;
Water fountains and roses red;
Green landscaped lawns unlimited.

A winding path that wends its way;
A water garden on display;
A shady ivy-covered nook
That beckons by a lazy brook.

Beyond the garden gate exist
Scenes that are by beauty kissed.
Peace and restful dreams await
Just beyond the garden gate.

Was it not Fate . . .

That bade me pause before

that garden gate

To breathe the incense of

those slumbering roses?

—Edgar Allan Poe

Roses tumble across an arbor in Martha's Vineyard, Massachusetts. Photo by William H. Johnson/Johnson's Photography.

Half-Past Spring

Mary E. Rathfon

Oh, could we turn to spring's first dawn,
And to its cheer with winter gone.
Back to the day when we first found
Buds bursting through the frosty ground;
When lovely yellow daffodils
And jonquils showed their lacy frills;
When tulips nodded to the notes
Which came from nesting robin throats;
When grass-tinged violets seemed to be
A green and purple tapestry;
And, like the climax of a play,
Fruit trees sent forth their grand display.

Time hurries, and we have no power
To turn it back for one brief hour.
So we must wait for next spring's dawn
When one more winter has passed on.

But still, it's only half-past spring.
More flowers will bloom; more birds will sing.
Each day will be a special one
Which brings new joys as time goes on,
And when spring turns to summer's charms,
We'll welcome them with open arms.

Ivy and spring blossoms adorn the base of a tree in Louisville, Kentucky. Photo by Daniel Dempster.

Readers' Forum

Snapshots from Our Ideals Readers

Above: Grandparents Rick and Sandy Remmert of Champaign, Illinois, tell us that ten-month-old Sophie Anne Remmert always wakes up happy from her naps, especially when she shares them with her favorite toy giraffe, Geno. Sophie is the daughter of Lynn and Dave Remmert of Monticello, Illinois.

Top right: Thirteen-month-old Bralyn Fox-Smith seems quite pleased with the colorful bow she is donning. Bralyn's snapshot was sent to us by her proud grandmother, Edith Fox of Refugio, Texas.

Lower right: Theo Cusato of Ellwood City, Pennsylvania, tells *Ideals* that her first great-granddaughter, Vanessa Huth, knows that a lady is never really well dressed without a hat on her head.

Top left: Sara, Patrick, and Erin Brigman will always have at least two good friends nearby to play with. The adorable triplets are the great-grandchildren of Lillian Brigman of Edenton, North Carolina.

Middle left: Judy Oldridge of Briercrest, Saskatchewan, Canada, sent us this picture of her first granddaughter, Chanel Lane Evans, age eleven weeks. Judy says that she is looking forward to tea parties and long walks with Chanel Lane in the years to come.

Lower left: Eight-month-old Sevryn Snow was visiting his great-grandmother, Bonnie Wunder, in Lake Park, Iowa, when he discovered a baby in the mirror that was somehow just as cute as he. Bonnie tells us she was thrilled to capture Sevryn's expression on film.

THANK YOU Rick and Sandy Remmert, Edith Fox, Theo Cusato, Lillian Brigman, Judy Oldridge, Bonnie Wunder, Eunice Mays, Hazel Doub, and Bonnie Will for sharing your family photographs with *Ideals*. We hope to hear from other readers who would like to share snapshots with the *Ideals* family. Please include a self-addressed, stamped envelope if you would like the photos returned. Keep your original photographs for safekeeping and send duplicate photos along with your name, address, and telephone number to:

Readers' Forum
Ideals Publications
535 Metroplex Drive, Suite 250
Nashville, Tennessee 37211

ideals

Publisher, Patricia A. Pingry
Editor, Michelle Prater Burke
Managing Editor, Peggy Schaefer
Designer, Marisa Calvin
Production Manager, Travis Rader
Copy Editor, Amy Johnson
Editorial Assistant, Patsy Jay
Contributing Editors, Lansing Christman,
Pamela Kennedy, Nancy Skarmeas, and Lisa Ragan

ACKNOWLEDGMENTS

BURKET, GAIL BROOK. "Humble Parent" and "To My Child." Reprinted by permission of Anne E. Burket. CROWELL, GRACE NOLL. "The Mothers of the Earth." Reprinted by permission of Claire Cumberworth. HOLMES, MARJORIE. "Mother's Apron" from *You and I and Yesterday*. Copyright © 1973 and renewed 1987 by Marjorie Holmes. Published by Doubleday Broadway Publishing. Used by permission of the author. HOLMES, REGINALD. "Spring Sonnet." Reprinted by permission of Shirley A. Radwick. RICHARDSON, ISLA PASCHAL. "When Lilacs Bloom" from *Against All Time*. Copyright © 1957 by Bruce Humphries, Inc. Used by permission of Branden Publishing Company, Inc. THOMAS, ESTHER KEM. "Mother's Day." Reprinted by permission of Frederick A. Thomas. VIORST, JUDITH. "Some Things Don't Make Any Sense At All" from *If I Were in Charge of the World and Other Worries*. Copyright © 1981 by Judith Viorst. Reprinted with the permission of Atheneum Books for Young Readers, an imprint of Simon & Schuster Children's Publishing Division. Our sincere thanks to the following authors whom we were unable to locate: Anne Campbell for "The Eye of the Beholder"; Lucille M. Crumley for ""Little Girl"; Elizabeth B. Estes for "Grandbaby"; Edith Helstern for "In the Shadows of an Attic"; Osman Castle Hooper for "The Old Lilac Bush"; Edna Jaques for "There Is So Much to Do"; Kim Konopka for "Small Offerings"; Douglas Malloch for "He's Got a Girl"; and Mildred Maralyn Mercer for "A Tribute to Grandmother."

Above: At his young age, Nathan Michael Saettel knows the value of a good friend, even in the tub. Nathan is the great-grandson of Eunice Mays of Louisville, Kentucky.

Below: Great-grandmother Hazel Doub of Tobaccoville, North Carolina, shares this photograph of her double delights: Lauren and Jordan Trivette. The twin sisters are three months old here and ready to play.

Below: Bonnie Will of Lebanon, Pennsylvania, shares this snapshot of her grandson, Matthew Ryan Cherry. After a valiant attempt, Matthew wasn't quite able to finish every morsel.